63 NATURAL REMEDIES TO STRESS & DEPRESSION WITH A-Z OF HAPPINESS

I0417156

Free and Easiest Ways to Conquer Stress, Depression & Achieving Happiness through NATUREWAS

63 NATURAL REMEDIES TO STRESS & DE PRESSION WITH A-Z OF HAPPINESS

JOHN ZEDGENBROTH JOE

Theologian and Psychologist

(University Of Arusha-Tanzania, Spicer College and University of Maharshi Dayanand, India)

Master of Psychology (University of Maharshi Dayanand, India)

Official Website: johnzedgenbrothjoe.weebly.com

: johnjoe.simdif.com

Email: sharegodslove.withhischildren@gmail.com

Copyright © September 2014-**John Zedgenbroth Joe**

First Edition

ISBN: 9781514170816

ABOUT THE AUTHOR

John Zedgenbroth Joe (Mwaniki) popularly known by his nickname as (Prime) is a New 21st Century young Theologian, Writer, Poet, Researcher and Psychologist. He is known as the first and youngest Psychologist in the world ever known to discover **HMQ** and **MC/MMC Testing** (On Moral Intelligence and Mind Compatibility especially for every couple before their Marriage). He is also accredited to **Psychemoanalysis** a field in psychology related to Freud's Psychoanalysis.

His classic and inspirational writings have touched and changed many lives of people in different countries. He enthusiastically loves to study about people's mind and come up with new science of mind. He is the author of the popular books *"The Secrets Of A Woman's Mind, Mental Health & Happiness," "Woman's Mind Innermost Hidden Secrets," "Women's Precious Fountain Of Well-being and Happiness," "Your Mind Opener," "60 Natural Remedies to Guilt, Anxiety, Sleep Loss & Sadness," "63 Natural Remedies to Stress and Depression with A-Z of Happiness," and "How It All Just Began"* the books which have transformed many people around the globe.

He is highly much in love with psychology and theology books writing and poetry. He builds new dreams every day and work to achieve them by the hand of God. He is much motivated by a one verse from the bible in the book of **Philippians 4:13** "I can do all things through Christ who strengthens me." His works will be remembered by all generations forever.

AUTHOR REVIEW

The bestselling author of "60 Natural Remedies to Guilt, Anxiety, Sleep loss and Sadness" and "How It All Just Began."

GENERAL EDITORIAL REVIEW

Many people are suffering from Stress. Others are going through depression in life, which make their current lives a misery. Due to many burdens in life, some are not even able to sleep or lack enough sleep. Some are sad in life, they live a life of regretting, pains, discomforts. Nothing seem good in life. You have tried all ways in life, but not even one is working. But even though life seem like a fiery, and not even one thing seems to cool it, still there is one more special and unique way left which can turn your life in to a laugher and joy and according to John Zedgenbroth Joe it's "The NATURE." Nature provides us with a wonderful atmosphere to help us carry many burdens in life. This is a volume on how to rely on nature in order to achieve a complete health especially by conquering Stress and Depression through a concept he termed as "NATUREWAS" and eventually attaining an ultimate happiness in your life. The book is written with a lot of skills which are easy to apply focusing on nature.

BOOK REVIEW

A classic Zedgenbroth Joe's Bestselling book on how to utilize nature in conquering Stress, Depression and Suicide and achieving an ultimate health and wellbeing. Zedgenbroth Joe is a young psychologist who has gone into a deeper study and discovered that nature can be used as a Psychological treatment to Stress, Depression Suicide Prevention. He uses beautiful terms like ", Sky walk, Psycho hydrotherapy" etc. meaning use of sky and water as natural therapies to treatment of psychological problems. Very excellent book from a talented author.

DEDICATED TO:

My beloved brother Robert Gitonga Joe and His Family, for his and their tender care of me in the absence of my late parents.

TO THE READER (PREFACE)

Stress is one of the topper causes of major diseases like high blood pressure, heart attack and many others. Together with depression, which is the main cause of suicide, both are the two main causes of many deaths in this generation.

In daily life I face a mass number of people suffering from Stress. Some are going through stress from the family relations, work tensions, diseases and many more. Others are going through depressions due to various reasons. These are very hot paths of depressions due to loss of loved ones, broken relationships, infidelity from their husband, pornography and many more. Others are in the point of suicide, to diminish themselves from troubles of this world.

But in spite of all this, everyone can still achieve their wellbeing and happiness. But the question is, how?

This volume of book carries numerous natural remedies to achieving all these and many more. In this book you will learn many causes of human discomforts, sadness, mental disturbances, and many more things causing everyone to spend their lives stressed, depressed, committing suicide, hence they are sad and unhappy in their lives. Eventually you are going to find in this book many many natural ways you can use to avoid them, free from them, conquer them and finally achieve an ultimate mental health naturally and free without any cost.

Finally or eventually, you will find a new concept in achieving a compete health and happiness through what I termed NATUREWAS. Since this is a book on how to rely on nature to be healthy and especially conquering stress and depression you will learn many natural ways you can be more and more healthier in life and hence becoming happier and happier in life.

The fact is that nature can help us accomplish many things even what we may think are unattainable or unachievable.

I believe that this book will finally or eventually give all human beings their minds and spirits a resting place and the atmosphere of ease feeling and beauty of special happiness. The things prescribed here are from day today life and they are practical and easy to do freely without any cost. Thank God for giving us free nature to dwell in, cure our ailments and diseases and even becoming happier in life every day.

Many have tried and they have achieved their complete mental health and ultimate happiness.

Why don't you try today and achieve your complete health and well being hence happier in life.

John Zedgenbroth Joe

GENERAL LAYOUT OF THE BOOK

CHAPTER 1

INTRODUCTION

Chapter Summary

Stress, Depression And Suicide

The Pain Of Stress, Depression And Suicide

The Essence Of Nature

The Beauty About the Nature

What involves the Nature

What is Natural Remedies

The Origin Of Natural Remedies

Application of Remedies in this Book

Is there another main focus of Nature apart from Healing?

Why Did I write this book?

Other Secrets about Nature

STRESS, DEPRESSION AND SUICIDE

Ｗe are all living in a world of stress and depression. Stress has become one of many peoples troubler in life. Everyone is going through a certain tension in life. Stress is one of the biggest obstacles which are arising from all corners in life. After family quarrels there is tension, after relationship break ups there is tension, too much work there is tension, when sick there is tension, when no money there is tension, when lose our loved ones there is tension, exam failures there is tension. Tension or stress is arising from all areas in life. And many people are finding it hard to cope up with it since they do not have a strong or firm foundation to rebel or conquer it.

On the other hand, depression is one of the major causes of many suicides today. Depression has attacked many people leaving them hopeless without a solution on what to do in life. The same areas in life causing stress or tension are in many ways the same ways causing depression. Starting from the family quarrels, broken relationships, work, education, lack of money, sicknesses and many more.

THE PAIN OF STRESS, DEPRESSION AND SUICIDE

It is true that we live in the world of calamities, mourning, anguish, devastations, hatred, depression, stress, infidelities, betrayals and death. Every day is troubles and tears from many many areas of life. Some are going through stress from the family relations, work tensions, diseases and many more. Some are passing through hot paths of depressions due to loss of loved ones, broken relationships, infidelity from their husband, pornography and many more. Others wish to end their lives due to every day troubles. Life is painful to many people, and even more painful when no one to turn to. It is like a burning fiery in a bush. It is so agonizing, anguishing, torturing, distressing, and tormenting.

These pains are unavoidable to many, no solutions to them, until many have ended up losing hope or value in their life. But my everyday life I wanted to say that, "Wherever there is a **Lock, there is a specific Key** for it." There is no problem that ever existed not even today, that hasn't been having a specific solution to it. Stress, depression and suicide are real life health threats and big problems to handle. But they have a solution.

There is an **ULTIMATE SOLUTION** to each of them. There is always a solution which has been existing around us. NATURE.

THE ESSENCE OF NATURE

Nature is **natural** and a **natural** way to conquering many obstacles and devastations in life and eventually achieving a complete health including mental health.

Yes, we all can still achieve mental health and happiness. All men and women including children can prevent themselves from stress, and overcome stress when it comes. They can conquer depression and overcome it. We all can overcome suicide. We all can stand up and fight against pornography---the present day marriages major stressor and killer.

The question you must be asking now is, "How can this happen in this painful and restless world? Or how can I be happy again after losing my husband, boyfriend, dad, mother, sister, brother? How can I be happy again after being cheated by my husband or my partner? How can I be happy again after now I got divorced?

How can I be free from stress which is part of my daily life? Or how can I conquer depression which is part of my life all this long? Or how can I stop myself from suicidal thinking?

It looks hard to achieve that right? But I want to tell you it is the easiest thing to do in this world. But how?

This volume of book carries numerous remedies prescribed from nature to conquering stress, depression and suicide for achieving all these and many more. In this book you will learn many causes of human discomforts, sadness, mental disturbances, and many more things causing all to spend their lives stressed, depressed, in slavery, and hence unhappy in their lives and eventually you will see many many natural ways you can use to avoid them, free from them, conquer them and finally achieve an ultimate mental health naturally and free without any cost.

The volume also moves on to explaining many ways we all can be happier in life. Through living a stress free, depression free, suicidal thoughts free, and many more in order to be able to achieve the ultimate freedom and eventually achieving the most precious fountain of happiness in all stages of their lives.

THE BEAUTY ABOUT THE NATURE

I want to say that **"Nature** is **Nurture."** It is capable of nourishing and nurturing the creation. The creation here means all things which God created including the nature itself. The nature then is meant to ensure that living things which are part of creations are nurtured and nourished to ensure their facilitation of their wellbeing. And hence nature is meant to nurture human being, by protecting, securing, nourishing and preventing human from many dangers in life including diseases.

WHAT INVOLVES THE NATURE

Nature involves all natural things like sun, moon, stars, sky, clouds, trees, rivers and water, fruits, vegetables, nuts and many more. The nature surrounds us and acts as our guards every day.

In addition, human beings are part of nature including, songs, reading word of God, animals, birds, grass, lakes, oceans, beaches, seas, exercise, tour, mountain climbing, swimming and many many more comprise the nature.

Hence, the word nature is quite broad enough to cover many God's created things.

WHAT IS NATURAL REMEDIES

Natural remedies are ways in which you can utilize the nature to benefit you in solving your problems. This benefit can be

- ✓ Preventing against a disease
- ✓ Curing
- ✓ Healing
- ✓ Securing
- ✓ Nourishing
- ✓ Supplementing
- ✓ Counseling
- ✓ Directing
- ✓ Pleasing
- ✓ And many more.

In most cases, when a word remedy is used, is meant to mean treatment of a disease. But as we have seen, remedy means more than treating. It encompasses, many areas in life which are useful or contribute to wellbeing of people.

THE ORIGIN OF NATURAL REMEDIES

Natural remedies can be traced back since the creation of this universe. I just want to say that when God was creating this universe; the sky, heavens, earth, living and non livings had a plan to do so. God had a purpose and plans for creating human being. And one of the plans of was sustaining and protection of human being. When He created in Genesis 1, He commanded the man and woman to bear children and spread over the universe, fill the earth and subdue it. But the question is, ' How could they subdue and fill the earth, live in it day by day without food?' Hence, God in Genesis 1, blessed them and gave them fruits from trees, vegetable from the gardens, nuts and many more as food.

This is the beginning of naturopath. God gave them these foods to feed, for outliving them and as well as to protect them from diseases. The same food, in combination with

✓ Water from the garden

- ✓ Exercise in a day
- ✓ Good relationship with each other
- ✓ Animals
- ✓ Plants and trees
- ✓ Resting or sleep
- ✓ Fresh air in the garden of Eden
- ✓ The sunlight which had been created earlier
- ✓ And many more,

were to be their **doctor** daily and, therefore, we see these people even living longer even up to **almost thousand years**. This is because they had allowed themselves to be part of nature and as well as utilizing the nature in solving many problems in their lives in addition to God.

But what happened, nowadays we live shorter and the life is even more in abundance with diseases? It is because we human beings have disobeyed God starting from His one of his first commandments found in Genesis 1.

➢ "To feed and completely rely on nature and God."

Many have wondered on the paths of feeding on flesh and animal products which was not God's original intension of creating human to feed on.

We should, therefore, return and utilize the nature and prevent ourselves from many dangers in life like diseases and pains of stress, depression etc.

APPLICATION OF REMEDIES IN THIS BOOK

This volume of book carries numerous natural remedies to help you conquer and or prevent yourself from stress, depression and suicide. In this book you will learn many causes of human discomforts, sadness, mental disturbances, and many more things causing all to spend their lives in pain of stress, depression, suicide, and hence unhappy in their lives and eventually you will see many many natural ways you can use to

- ✓ Avoid them,
- ✓ Free from them,
- ✓ Conquer them and finally
- ✓ Achieve an ultimate mental health naturally and free without any cost.

By achieving mental health is the ultimate and safe journey of achieving happiness. And by achieving happiness, is an ultimate safe journey to a life of betterment and great and secure success. 'Great and Secure Success' or **GSS** here means success which you can be happy in. Some people are rich in life and still successful, but are not happy in life. This I term as 'Small and Insecure Success' or **SIS**. It is insecure because one cannot celebrate his success because is full of stress or depression.

God's unique purpose for our life is to depend in Him and nature and eventually acquire **GSS** in life.

IS THERE ANOTHER MAIN FOCUS OF NATURE APART FROM HEALING?

There is more to have from nature apart from prevention and healing. The volume also moves on to explaining many ways we all can be **happier** in life. Through living a stress free, depression free, suicidal thoughts free, and able to achieve the ultimate happiness. Hence there is another main focus on nature and this is Happiness.

If we can look at the book of Revelation the bible, the last chapters about new heavens and new earth;

- A river and
- Water of life
- A tree of life on each side of the river
- 12 crops of fruit and
- A fruit every month
- Leaves of the tree are for healing of nations

This means that God will have restored the earth to as it was in Garden of Eden. This is a **hint** to tell all of us that in the new heaven no need of priests and medical doctors any more for **THE LAMB OF GOD** and the **NATURE** will serve that. And this is also a hint that **happiness** which will be forever facilitated by nature (e.g. River of life, Tree of life, Healing leaves) in that there will be;

- ✓ No more Death
- ✓ No more mourning
- ✓ No more crying
- ✓ No more Pain
- ✓ For the old order of things has passed away.

What am trying to say is that nature since the beginning is not only meant for healing and prevention but also for Happiness and this will be even in the NEW EARTH.

WHY DID I WRITE THIS BOOK?

As both Theologian and Psychologist, I see every day people suffering from stress, depression and others committing suicide and hence unhappy in life. Others have reached a point of giving up in life. They have tried much but they never find any help. But after applying nature in my life, I find very significant changes in my health and life, and eventually, I find lots of happiness in solving many problems through nature and I feel I should share my benefits with someone else.

This book I wrote it to be all human kinds' **resting place** and a place they can **free** themselves from many day today dangers and threats of their lives. When dangers come in life someone can run into this book and find a resting place for his or her life troubles through applying easy to do natural keys to open the room for more happiness in his or her life.

Eventually, giving you the atmosphere of **ease feeling** and **beauty** of **special happiness and joy.** The things prescribed here are from day today life and they are easy to do freely without any cost.

Do them every day and you will find your life in lots of happiness and joy from people, nature and God.

Eventually, you find yourself asking, "How did I make it to all this never ending precious river of joy and happiness?"

OTHER SECRETS ABOUT NATURE

This is practical volume of book which carries numerous natural remedies to stress, depression and suicide and ultimately giving you a better and a new journey to a never ending happiness. In this book you will learn many causes of human discomforts, like what causes stress, depression, and suicide in daily life.

Eventually, you are going to find in this book many many natural ways you can use to avoid them, free from them, conquer them and finally achieve an ultimate mental health naturally and free without any cost. The nature has the ability to bring many changes in your life;

- ✓ **Transforming** you
- ✓ **Reforming** you and eventually gives you a
- ✓ **Resting** place for all your burdens so that you can be
- ✓ **Free** and **happier** in life.

CHAPTER 2

STRESS

Chapter Summary

What Is Stress?

Gender and Stress

Symptoms and Signs of Stress
1. Physical and Medical Symptoms
2. Behavioral and Social Symptoms
3. Psychological and Cognitive Symptoms
4. Feelings and Emotional Symptoms

The Major Stressors to Human
1. Work Related Stressors
2. Relationships Stressors
3. Health Related Stressors
4. Finance Related Stressors
5. Stressors from Nature
6. Other Stressors
   A. Education/Studies Stress
   B. Religious Related Stressors
   C. All Kinds of Discriminations
   D. Unsafe Environment Stressors

WHAT IS STRESS?

S tress is a normal physical and or mental or emotional response to some or many events that make you feel tensioned and sometimes threatened or sad. Stress is any tension which leads to over working or under working of mental processes like thinking.

I can also define it as a pressure which results from outward exerted forces and which lowers or increases mental processes. Those outward forces can be excess work, sickness, poor or broken relationships and many more. One fact about these external forces is that they lead to body pressure or stress and this pressure affects all other body process. Hence with stress, one might also be diagnosed with another disorder or disease.

Research have shown that like when you perceive a threat, your nervous system might respond by releasing a number of stress hormones, like adrenaline which in turn wakes your body for emergency action. This may lead your heart beating faster, muscles tightening, blood pressure rising up, and your breath quickens.

GENDER AND STRESS

It is good we look at the gender and see which is at a higher risk. Men or women? Women seem to suffer from Stress more than men. This is true as I have mentioned in my book "Woman's Mind Innermost Hidden Secrets." Women have thinker **hippocampus** as compared to men which involved in learning, memory and emotions.

Hence women are more emotional than men. This means that a very small negative thing may lead to a woman thinking a lot and deeply unhappy. Due to this structural and functional difference in mind may lead to more stress in women than in men.

According to recent researches most of those who suffer from stress are women. According the survey which I carried in India, recently, about 7 to 8 out of 10 women are going through stress often in their life due to different troubles in life.

SYMPTOMS AND SIGNS OF STRESS

1. Physical and Medical Symptoms

- Feeling dizzy
- Sometime diarrhea
- Sometimes constipation
- Nausea
- Sometimes heartbeat increases
- Some people lose sex drive.

2. Behavioral and Social Symptoms

- Some people may stay without eating
- Some people sleeping too much and some uneasy to
- sleep
- Some isolate themselves
- Stress leads to poor working conditions and
- Neglecting responsibilities
- Some starts drinking and smoking and use other
- Drugs
- Biting of nails in some people.

3. Psychological and Cognitive Symptoms

- Constant worrying
- Seeing only the negative
- Memory problems
- Poor thinking
- Poor judgment
- Poor and wrong perceptions
- Low self efficacy
- Bad mood
- Etc.

4. Feelings and Emotional Symptoms

- Feeling unhappy
- Feeling irritating
- Sadness on the face
- Feeling alone
- Crying (in some cases)
- Etc.

The most common stress areas in human's life are the areas which am going to discuss here and, thereafter, provide effective good and free cost psychotherapies and ultimate guidelines and remedies toward all of them.

1. Work Related Stressors

Work stress is the top stressor in many countries. In the US, about 70 % of workers report that they experience stress in work. These stressors might arise from one or all of the following;

- When not happy in your job especially compared to your salary.
- Too much work or heavy work.
- Over time
- Lack of security at work
- Being given extra responsibilities
- Work discrimination
- Being harassed
- Etc.

2. Relationships Stressors

This is the second stressor many people are facing daily. In my research recently, I have come across many women who are not happy with their lives. After asking them the reason, more than 80% reasons fall on relationship failures.

The main relationship stressors are:

- The death of a loved one
- Divorce
- Loss of a husband (Window)
- Sex related issues
- Infidelity
- Breakage with a loved one
- Lack of someone to marry
- Etc.

3. Health Related Stressors

This is the third stressor in life. Many people when they are diagnosed with a certain disease they are ending up being distressed with themselves. These diseases are like;

- Asthma
- Bronchitis
- Cancer

- Diabetes
- STDs
- Heart Diseases
- Etc.

The victims of these kinds of diseases may start over thinking which might lead to stress and this stress may lead to anxiety which if not diagnosed and treated on time might lead to depression. Other people also get stressed indirectly, just because they have a patient who is sick.

4. Finance Related Stressors

This is the fourth stressor in life. It involves lack of money or enough money to accomplish some tasks in life.

It includes;

- Lack of job
- Earning little salary
- Having to pay more to your children fees
- No rent
- Poverty
- Etc.

5. Stressors from Nature

This is the fifth stressor in life. It involves;

- Fear
- Worries or anxiety about the future
- Uncertainty
- How you perceive the world in most cases in a negative way
- Stressed about people's sins also I call it **self-stress** because it involves taking burdens of others. For example if people are much involved in so many sins, you may get unhappy and become stressed over it
- Failed expectations or hope
- Etc.

6. Other Stressors

A. Education/Studies Stress

Most of students get stress when get a lot of assignments, long syllabus and when nearing exams. A lot of work leads to overload of mental processes leading to stress. Due to overload of study work, they sleep late night which does not give

amygdala (a brain part involved in memory processing) enough time to even process the leaned information. This leads to poor performance in class. Students hence should try and have enough sleep at night.

B. Religious Related Stressors

These stressors come as a result of being much involved in religious work like preaching, conversion of people etc. It might be highly experienced by pastors, priests, prophets etc.

C. All Kinds of Discriminations

These come as a result of discrimination or bad treatment of people's denying even freedom. Discrimination of people or mistreatment of other persons may lead to stress.

D. Unsafe Environment Stressors

These can come as a result of poor relationship with the neighboring people. There some neighbors who are very disturbing nature. Neighbor here may not only refer to person living next to your door but also family members, neighboring countries, neighboring states etc.

CHAPTER 3

18 NATURAL REMEDIES TO STRESS

Chapter Summary

Suffering From Stress?

The 18 Effective Natural Remedies and Psychotherapies To All Kinds Of Stresses

SUFFERING FROM STRESS?

Stress has been one of the major problems facing almost every one today. Many people haven't been able to recover the immediate ways they can help themselves from the nature. But following these natural remedies given here will help you to avoid stress, manage your stress when you face it and as well as to add your happiness to the peak. The remedies are prescribed from the nature. Use them carefully or strictly and they will surely help you.

THE 18 EFFECTIVE NATURAL REMEDIES AND PSYCHOTHERAPIES TO ALL KINDS OF STRESSES

Relaxation

1. Just Relax and have some funs

Relaxing means you should not think too much about the issue. Sit down and figure out the issue and how you can solve it. Then try to have funs. Having funs means you can think of making a joke with someone or thinking of going to the beach with your loved one. Please note that the fun should not lead you to immoral acts like drinking or casual sex. Always know the limit of your funs.

Also trying tensing tightly each part of your body and relaxing them afterwards, from the head, to the toes;

- Head muscles
- Face muscles
- Eye muscles by closing the eyelids tightly and opening
- Neck muscles
- Hands
- Fists
- Fingers
- Stomach
- Legs
- Knees
- Toes
- Etc.

After **tightly tensing** each part of the body separately for about 5 seconds, then relax. This remedy is quite effective when combined with remedy 2.

2. Have a Night Walk also called 'Sky Walk'

Having a walk alone and trying to breathe deeply in and out can reduce stress. This remedy is more effective when combined with remedy 1.

The best walk is usually at night. When you are slightly walking, look at the sky; the stars, moon, clouds and the beauty of heaven. This is very effective natural therapy for stress, which I call **'sky anti-stress'**. This has been my remedy over many years and it really works. To me it is one of the most effective natural remedies to stress. I termed it **sky walk** because I;

- Walk looking at the sky
- The moon
- The stars
- and clouds moving

and I feel the pleasure of walking in the stars indeed. This is done slowly walking looking at the sky and deeply breathing in and out. You may combine it with remedy 1 for more effectiveness. It's kind of a funny but it really help very much. Try it sometime and see.

3. Spend time in or with the nature

Try and visit natural places like;

- Rivers,
- Lakes,
- Mountains,
- Trees,
- Seas
- Beaches

And try to imagine being part of the nature, by participating with what that nature does. For example, if you visit a lake or a river, try and put your legs in the water, and feel the movements. This feeling get sensed by your legs and is sent to your brain through sensory nerves which may lead to ease feeling and joy in your brain.

If you visit a beach you may lie on the mud, that is, sleep on the side of the beach where the waters is arriving and getting back. Sleep on all sides (back, front, sides) for about 5 minutes at each time. This is also so effective remedy to stress. Do you know why? You are created from the mud!! The body you are having now is made from the dust +breath of life from God. Spend time in that mud. It may look crazy but you are getting healed.

This is what I call NATURE IMMERSING. It mixing yourself with nature to get relieved.

4. Call for a Good friend

Sharing your stress with someone you trust reduce your mind from stress with more than 50%. In other words this is one of the first things you should do when something big happens. Wherever you share the half of stress is gone. And you can then work with rest using these remedies.

5. Take a long cold bath

As I have just mentioned on nature (immersing) as a remedy, water do a lot to relieve one from stress. Take a long bath especially with cold water. As much as it may depend on you, spend more time in the water (fill a bathing tank with water in the bathroom). Usually there is a kind of special communication which takes place between water and your brain. Brain in nature is quite friendly with water and that's why those who suffer from chronic headaches or any other headaches are advised to drink a lot of water. Hence water I call it **'psychophilos'** meaning that you cannot separate the brain from water. They are strong friends.

6. Drink more warm water

Also drink more water especially warm in nature. It is also a good psychophilos to stress relief. Usually your brain require at least 20% of oxygen that you inhale. Why? Because brain is involved in serving and or controlling many activities 24 hours like;

- Breathing
- Heart beat,
- Thinking
- Reasoning
- Digestion
- Memory processing
- Decision making
- Memory storage
- Walking
- Balancing
- Coordination
- Temperature control
- Sleep
- Waking
- Hearing
- Sight
- Drinking
- Eating
- Sensing
- Etc.

These and many more activities are served and or controlled by the brain 24 hours. It hence requires enough energy to do so. This energy comes from food you eat. For the food to provide energy to the brain, OXYGEN is needed.

Now, why then need too much water especially when stressed? WATER is made up of Hydrogen and Oxygen i.e. ($H2 + \mathbf{O2} = H2O2$ [water]) In other words water ($H2O2$) contains oxygen in it and since the brain is in need of very high amount of oxygen especially when STRESSED, one should drink a lot of water to help the brain especially in reasoning and thinking especially now one is stressed. When one is stressed in many cases, brain is involved in many activities (e.g. thinking, reasoning) than normal

7. Get Foot Massage

Massaging can also do better especially on the feet as feet have a reflexes or have nerves which are direct to the brain. Try stimulating these nerves and can lead to a good feeling too.

8. Listen to a Nice Cooling Music

Music, especially religious songs which are played softly do a lot in relieving stress. Please be sure to select wisely the songs to play because some songs are stressors by themselves. For example listening to a rock song after losing your loved one may keep on adding your stress. Please play your music softly especially a spiritual song.

9. Watch a Funny video or a Comedy

Now watching a comedy will depend on what is stressing you. If it is something small like losing your phone or failure in exam, comedy may be good. This is because it might entertain you until your mind gets disconnected with the stressors for some time. Hence, feeling happier and better.

But for a bigger thing like losing a loved one it's better to listen to a cooling music. Funny video at this moment of time is not advisable and it may look like you don't bother losing your loved one. The cooling music should then be one which is;

- ✓ Encouraging
- ✓ Comforting
- ✓ Strengthening
- ✓ Giving you hope
- ✓ Or all of these especially spiritually.

10. Prefer Silent Place for a while and write down your feelings

When stressed, sit down and relax in the absence of noise and public. Silence is good for it will help to maintain your reasoning and try to figure out the way out of stress. Please note that silence here doesn't mean always. Just for a while and get into sharing with someone you trust.

At this moment, take a piece of paper and a pen, write down on the top of the paper, what is stressing you followed by what you feel. Write as much as you can. For example you may write on a piece of paper:

Title: *Am stressed of my relationship failure*

➤ I feel angry
➤ I feel like killing some one
➤ I feel like dying or killing myself
➤ I feel hopeless
➤ I feel worthless
➤ I feel empty without him/her
➤ I feel like the world is ending
➤ I feel not important any more
➤ I can't live without him/her
➤ I will never have a job
➤ I am going to die of this disease
➤ Etc

Ensure you write as much as you can. Then read what you have written at least 3 times. The more you write the more you reduce the stress. The more you read what you have written the more you are getting healed from the stress. **HOW?**

Try look at this table in this remedy 10 very carefully and assume you are the one who have written it on a piece of paper. Actually when you write, then you read something like what is on this table, you will abruptly be caught up with a laughter, you may laugh at yourself like a child. For example being stressed after being breaking up in a relationship, then assume you write on a piece of paper; *I feel like dying or killing myself or I can't live without him/her.* Then you read it again and again, you may come to realize that what is stressing you is not even necessary and laugh at yourself after realizing what is stressing you.

For example, *I feel like dying or killing myself*.

When you read this on your piece of paper you may ask yourself; **Killing myself just because of relationship failure?**

This remedy is so effective to stress and I term it as **graphogelio** natural remedy.

Graphogelio is a word made of two Greek words 'grapho' (write) and 'gelio' (laugh). Graphogelio means write and laugh. This is because in this remedy it is highly possible that after you write what is stressing you plus what you feel and read again and again, you will end up laughing at yourself.

11. Get enough Rest.

Please remember not to overwork yourself. If stressed have a break or if employed ask for a short leave in order to sit down rest your mind and figure out the stressor clearly. The second thing, to some people stress causes them not to have enough sleep. Ensure you go to your bed at the same time you are used to. Have enough sleep. Sleep helps a lot in relaxing your mind. The more you sleep the more the mind relaxes but also are careful not to oversleep.

12. Spend time with others

Spend time with positive people who influence your life positively. When you spend time with those people you will feel as if they are also sharing in your stress. Please be careful of the people you spend time with. Some might be more stressors than your current stress. Be selective especially in times like this.

Self Humor (I love myself)

13. Be humorous to yourself

The act of laughing helps your body fight stress in a number of ways. Get to your bedroom and laugh at yourself. Stand at the mirror and laugh with your mirror image. I love myself remedy involves 4 steps:

> 1. Stand in front of a big mirror.
> 2. Read the piece of paper you wrote on remedy 10 as you are standing on a big mirror and while recording with a recorder For example say loudly; *"I feel like dying or killing myself."*
> 3. Ensure you are looking at yourself on the mirror as you read it through the whole piece of paper.
> 4. Now, as you stand on the mirror open the recorder and listen to yourself as you are facing the mirror.

By listening to yourself, will cause you laughing at yourself. And since you are looking at yourself in front of the mirror, will ADD up the laughter.

This may sound crazy but it reduces stress with high capacity. I call it **'self humor' or "I love myself'** stress remedy because it's funny and it shows how you love yourself and that you love to be happy. Next thing you find is laughing like a crazy person but you aren't. Actually you are becoming better. This is very effective natural remedy to stress and I use it and laugh at myself and makes my day.

This remedy can be used even when not stressed to add up your happiness.

Exercise

14. Go for an exercise in the field

Exercise is one of the effective remedies to stress but it is more effective when is preceded by a Sky Walk I have discussed in my stress remedy number 2. Exercise regularly and even do it more especially when you are stressed. If you love gym, it might be good. Also walking around your garden or outside your house quietly may help a lot.

15. Adopt Healthy Eating Lifestyle

Some people when stressed do not eat enough or never eat at all as I have indicated in the behavioral symptom in this chapter. It is important you eat as usual. Start with breakfast. Eat enough breakfast, full of fiber with legumes, vegetable, nuts and collection of fruits. Eat enough like a big manager as if you are in the Garden of Eden. Please avoid at all coffee, tea, alcohol, bear, whine, sugar and any other caffeine related substances. These do a lot of harm to your body and may affect your sleep. Avoid alcohol, even though is rarely. It promotes stress.

Take fresh fruits or vegetables or both fruits and vegetables juice. Make juice by yourself. Get collection of fruits, vegetables and juicer and make your own juice. This is very nice especially when suffering from stress or depression.

Why? As I said in remedy no. 6, brain is involved in many activities and these activities are served and or controlled by the brain 24 hours. It hence requires enough energy to do so. This energy comes from food you eat. When stressed it is, therefore, very important you eat food which can be BROKEN DOWN to produce energy as fast as possible. This can be like fresh fruit juice which requires less or no digestion to be absorbed and taken to the brain areas especially the frontal lobe.

You should therefore, make juice by yourself which contains all nutrients so that to help the brain in this time of higher activity (stress).

It is like a car. The faster you drive, the faster the car consumes fuel right? Yea!! What I mean here is that give brain something which can be broken down into energy so fast like fresh fruit juice. Take some few glasses like 3, 4, or even 5 of fresh fruit juice when in stress.

16. Avoid Watching Stressing Movies

Avoid watching stressing movies like action movies. They are also stress promoters. Some may be carrying stress related scenes. For example if you are stressed because you have broken up in a relationship, watching a romantic movie or comedy may add up stress which may even lead to depression. The fact is that when you watch your mind starts relating your previous memories, how you were in deep love, how you enjoyed your relationship but eventually breaking up and that would hurts you at watching. Avoid stressors by avoiding the stress related movies.

17. Change your Standard Procedure

This means that if you are used to eat dinner or lunch at home, this stressing moment you may think of going out for dinner in a hotel with a friend. This will motivate you to a new way of life rather than you are used to. This will also prevent you from staying in one place hence reducing stress.

18. Trust in God and meditate about Him

Another thing visit worship places most of times. Trust in God of heaven and Jesus. In case you may need to know more about Jesus, please visit any church and ask anyone to tell you more about Him. He is the greatest helper in times of stress and problems and He can restore back your happiness.

God is our Creator and sustainer and He understands all our problems. In this case when stressed spend a quality time **meditating** about your spiritual life. Think about God, pray and do even sing a song. Sing any song which is related to God, even though you may not know any song, you can just say, **"thank you God for everything in my life."**

CHAPTER 4

DEPRESSION AND SUICIDE

Chapter Summary .

What Is Depression?

Who is At HigHer Risk

Signs and Symptoms of Depression

Suicidal Attempts

Depressions Disorders
   1. Major Depressive Disorder
      Diagnosis of Major Depressive Disorder
   2. Dysthymia
      Diagnosis of Dysthymia
   3. Bipolar Disease Also Manic Depressive Disorder
      Diagnosis of Bipolar

Depression can be defined as a disorder that involves the mind, body, and emotions, and that affects the way a person acts, eats, drinks, sleeps, feels about himself or herself, and other things includes life in general. Depression sometimes is confused with stress but these two disorders are different. Stress is just a short term tension or a temporary pressure while depression is vice versa that is long term in nature. For example a person who commits suicide in many cases is as a result of depression but not stress.

One similarity between stress and depression is that both lower mental processes like thinking, reasoning, and sometimes increase them etc. A person with either stress or depression may not perform well in exam as compared to somebody who is normal.

Another thing about depression is that if it cannot get diagnosed on time, it may continue for weeks, months and even years.

Just as in the case of stress, women seem to suffer from depression more than men. This might be as a result of the structural and functional differences between man's and woman's brain. Women have thick **hippocampus** which is involved in learning, memory and emotions. Hence women are more emotional than men. This means that a very small negative thing may lead to a woman thinking a lot and deeply unhappy. This structural and functional difference in mind may lead to more depression in women than in men.

However, women have more **Oxytocin** as compared to men, which help them to connect easily and share their problems with other women. In addition women have more **Seroton** which when combined with Oxytocin plus Estrogen can help women to connect easily and be less aggressive as seen today.

Hence, though women are at a higher risk, they are able to escape the depression faster than men.

Once one is depressed he may have changes especially loosing interests in the following kinds of activities and show many symptoms like;

- Not feeling like eating
- He may eat more than usual
- He may gain more or because of eating too much
- He may lose wait
- Lose sex appetite
- Become sad
- Get worried
- Feels worthless
- Loose hope
- He may feel guilt of his past which may add up the pain
- Worthlessness
- Helplessness
- Doesn't speak to people
- Sleep failure
- Too much sleep
- Feeling restless
- He or she might have headaches many times
- And finally he may even opt for suicide.

Suicide is referred to as a self-termination of life through physical or chemical means like hanging and taking poison in order to die. The thoughts of suicide are experienced by someone who has in most cases gone through a depression for a very long time. When depression goes for a long period without being diagnosed or treated, all the above symptoms finally lead to a feeling of unworthiness and one feels is unworthy.

In a country like India where most of my research has been founded, most of suicidal cases are committed by young girls. In most cases due to love issues like;

➢ Break ups
➢ Relationship tensions
➢ Parents denial for acceptance she marries the person she loves
➢ And many more.

The feeling of unworthiness finally leads to one thinking of suicide.

DEPRESSIONS DISORDERS

Now, let's look at some types of depressions disorders. There are three main depression disorders namely;

- Major Depression (Major Depressive disorder)
- Dysthymia
- Bipolar Disease also Manic Depressive Disease.

1. Major Depressive Disorder

Major depressive disorder is also called **Unipolar depression** and is characterized by a pervasive and persistent low mood with low self-esteem and of course loss of interest especially the one I have listed above like lack of appetite and lack of sex drives.

This disorder also called MDD may eventually affect a person's family, friends, work, and school life, eating, and sleeping. This later affects the rest of one's health.

According to the recent researches approximately 3 to 4% of the US with major depression commits suicide. About 55 to 60% of people who commit suicide had depression or another mood disorder.

MDD may be diagnosed through;

- Observed symptoms
- Patient's self-reported feelings
- Friend or relatives reports
- Psychiatrist or Clinical Psychologist examination
- Physician examination
- DSM (IV)
- Questionnaires and Inventories like Beck's
- Case History
- Clinical interview
- etc.

2. Dysthymia

The second disorder is called Dysthymia or Neurotic Depression or sometime called chronic disorder. This disorder just as MDD is a mood disorder consisting of similar symptoms though they are less severe and longer lasting.

It is a chronic depression in nature and may last for at least 2 years for adults and 1 year for children and teens. Due to its chronic in nature, as a result, the sufferers may end up believing that depression is a part of their character, and hence they may refuse to talk or discuss their symptoms with anyone including psychiatrists, clinical psychologists, doctors, family members, or even friends and relatives.

Diagnosis of Dysthymia

Just as MDD, Dysthymia can be diagnosed through;

- Patient's self-reported feelings
- Psychiatrist or Clinical Psychologist examination
- Friend or relatives reports
- Questionnaires and Inventories like Beck's
- Physician examination
- DSM (IV)
- Case History
- Clinical interview
- Observed symptoms
- etc.

3. Bipolar Disease Also Manic Depressive Disorder

This disorder is characterized by the following symptoms;

- Feeling sad and uneasy for at least 2 weeks
- You may find someone weeping for no reason
- Worthless feeling
- And some or all others symptoms of depression as I've listed in this chapter.

Diagnosis of Bipolar

Just as MDD and Dysthymia, Bipolar can be diagnosed through;

- DSM (IV)
- Case History
- Patient's self-reported feelings
- Psychiatrist or Clinical Psychologist examination
- Physician examination
- Questionnaires and Inventories like Beck's
- Clinical interview
- Observed symptoms
- Friend or relatives reports
- etc.

CHAPTER 5

22 NATURAL REMEDIES AND PSYCHOTHERAPIES FOR DEPRESSION AND SUICIDE PREVENTION

Chapter Summary

Are You Depressed In Life?

22 Effective Natural Remedies and Psychotherapies for Depression and Suicidal Prevention

Depression is a brother of Stress though the depth of experience of both is different. Depression just as Stress has been one of the attackers of many people today especially women. It is one of the major disorders facing almost every one today. Many people haven't been able to discover the immediate ways they can help themselves from the nature. But following these natural remedies given here will help you to

- ✓ Avoid depression very easily
- ✓ Manage it when you it comes
- ✓ Kick off Depression
- ✓ Say good bye to depression
- ✓ Help you prevent suicide and as well as to
- ✓ Add your happiness to the peak.

The remedies are prescribed from the nature. Use them carefully or strictly and they will surely help you.

2

1. Always be positive

Know always that suicide carries many death possibilities like suicide. Be calm always and try to be positive in all things. Always try and challenge the depression and suicidal thoughts by replacing them with a positive thinking or what I term as **Word Replacement Therapy (WRT).** For example, a Saying like "I am hated by all people!" can be replaced with "I am loved by all people or at least even though the world hates me, "GOD LOVES ME."

WRT involves first challenging your thoughts by replacing them with **positive thoughts.**

Secondly, look for support for your positive statement. For example, try and look for more evidence that you are loved than you are hated. For example, "Though my relationship is a failure I am loved because, at least that person accepted to come to my life at first, meaning that I am very important person." This is what I call Word Replacement Therapy (WRT) or Natural remedy or psychotherapy. It may also be called Sentence Replacement Therapy (SRT) when replacing negative thoughts sentences with positive thoughts sentences.

In addition, you can challenge poor thoughts of depression and suicide and achieve more positive thinking through **Positive Self Comparison Therapy (PSCT).**

Say that it's not only you who is going through that painful experience. There are many more in the world going through the same pain. No human can be happy always. Sometimes some pains come but with trust in God they wither away soon.

This is a Positive self comparison in that, you compare your miseries in life and consider them to be too small as compared to bigger miseries ever happened or happening to many people.

For example in the bible we have miseries of Job (Job chapter 1). Assume you have depression as a result of losing your son or daughter. Positive self comparison is that asking a question like; I LOST MY SON/DAUGHTER and am this depressed, WHAT ABOUT JOB WHO LOST ALL HIS CHILDREN? AND WHAT DID HE

SAY? "NAKED I CAME AND NAKED SHALL I RETURN, PRAISE BE THE NAME OF THE LORD.

Positive Self Comparison Therapy or PSCT is very effective remedy to depression as one feels is **at least better** with smaller misery he/she has at the moment as compared to those who had, have or are experiencing worse than that.

2. Self value yourself plus visit a Clinical Psychologist, Psychiatrist or medical doctor

Self value means you need to tell yourself that you are important. This can happen like using a video camera or standing in front of a mirror. When standing in front of the mirror or in front of a camera, say to the image on the mirror or video camera; "YOU ARE THE MOST IMOPRTANT PERSON IN THIS WORRLD." This is better if doing it smiling. (Remember actually, you are saying "You" but you mean "I." You are telling to yourself indirectly that you are important).

Also, as soon as possible, consult a depression health professional. The earlier you do this the better to avoid many negative symptoms.

3. Diarise your thoughts and write down

When you are depressed unless you put into a diary what you want to accomplish, you may find yourself forgetting many responsibilities. Having a diary arranging your responsibilities can help much to avoid missing into some of your obligations.

Secondly just as in the case of stress, at this moment, take a piece of paper and a pen, write down on the top of the paper, what is depressing you followed by what you feel. Write as much as you can. For example you may write on a piece of paper:

Title: *Am Depressed of my relationship failure*

➢ I feel angry
➢ I feel like killing some one
➢ I feel like dying or killing myself
➢ I feel hopeless
➢ I feel worthless
➢ I feel empty without him/her
➢ I feel like the world is ending
➢ I feel not important any more
➢ I can't live without him/her
➢ I will never have a job
➢ I am going to die of this disease
➢ Etc

Ensure you write as much as you can. Then read what you have written at least 3 times. The more you write the more you reduce the depression. The more you read what you have written the more you are getting healed from the depression. **HOW?**

Try look at this table in this remedy 3 very carefully and assume you are the one who have written it on a piece of paper. Actually when you write, then you read something like what is on this table, you will abruptly be caught up with laughter, you may laugh at yourself like a child. For example being depressed after being breaking up in a relationship, then assume you write on a piece of paper; *I feel like dying or killing myself or I can't live without him/her.* Then you read it again and again, you may come to realize that what is depressing you is not even necessary and laugh at yourself after realizing what is depressing you.

For example, *"I feel killing myself or just committing suicide and die."*

When you read this on your piece of paper you may ask yourself; **Killing myself just because of relationship failure?**

This remedy is so effective to both stress and depression and I termed it as **Graphogelio** natural remedy.

Graphogelio is a word made of two Greek words 'grapho' (write) and 'gelio' (laugh). Graphogelio means write and laugh. This is because in this remedy it is highly possible that after you write what is depressing you plus what you feel and read again and again, you will end up laughing at yourself.

4. Go for Work As Usual

Ensure you visit to your daily routines as you are used to. Do not fail to report to your daily work as usual. This is going to make you interact with others and they can make you feel important. Ensure you immerse yourself into all your responsibilities as usual. This ensures you are busy, and that doesn't give you a chance or time to have negative thinking hence lowering depression level. Ensure you are always busy especially at this time. Busy here does not mean watching TV or movie but means involving yourself into a higher level of muscular activity like;

- Cleaning your house
- Writing a book
- Chatting
- Being on phone
- Writing an article
- Playing with your kids, family members

➢ Etc.

5. Avoid Suicidal Thinking

Try always not to stay alone. Always think of mixing with others. When you mix with people, give no room for suicidal thinking. This will help you challenge the poor suicidal thoughts.

6. Change your Daily Leisure

This means that if you are used to go for evening leisure in the gym, you may today think of visiting your best friend. By changing your daily leisure time will motivate you to a new way of life rather than you are used to. This will also prevent you from staying in one place.

7. Keep going out with friends for dinner

As I have mentioned in the case of stress, just ensure you visit your close friend sometimes and try to share with him.

Sharing seems to help a lot. The more you feel like being alone, the more you need to think of going to someone for a company. Keep on going out with your friends.

8. Just Relax and have some funs

Just as in the case of stress relaxing means you should not think too much about the issue. Sit down and figure out the issue and how you can solve it. Then try to have funs. Having funs means you can think of making a joke with someone or thinking of going to the beach with your loved one. Just as I have mentioned in stress remedies, please note that the fun should not lead you to immoral acts like drinking or casual sex. Always know the limit of your funs.

Just as in stress, when depressed try tensing tightly each part of your body and relaxing them afterwards, from the head, to the toes;

- Head muscles
- Face muscles
- Eye muscles by closing the eyelids tightly and opening
- Neck muscles
- Hands
- Fists

- ❖ Fingers
- ❖ Stomach
- ❖ Legs
- ❖ Knees
- ❖ Toes
- ❖ Etc.

After **tightly tensing** each part of the body separately for about 5 seconds, then relax. This remedy just as in stress remedies is quite effective when combined with remedy 9 of depression.

9. Have a Night Walk also called 'Sky Walk'

Just as in stress case, having a walk alone and trying to breathe deeply in and out can reduce stress. This remedy is more effective when combined with remedy 8 of depression.

The best walk is usually at night. When you are slightly walking, look at the sky; the stars, moon, clouds and the beauty of heaven. This is very effective natural therapy for depression, which I called **'sky anti-stress.'** To me it is one of the most effective natural remedies to both stress and depression. I termed it **sky walk** because I;

- ❖ Walk looking at the sky
- ❖ The moon

❖ The stars

❖ and clouds moving

and I feel the pleasure of walking in the stars indeed. This is done slowly walking looking at the sky and deeply breathing in and out. You may combine it with remedy 8 for more effectiveness. It's kind of a funny but it really help very much. Try it sometime and see.

10. Spend time in or with the nature

Try and visit natural places like rivers, lakes, mountains, trees, try to imagine being part of the nature, by participating with what that nature does. For example, if you visit a lake or a river, try and put your legs in the water, and feel the movements. This feeling get sensed by your legs and is sent to your brain through sensory nerves which may lead to ease feeling and joy in your brain and your whole body.

Also if you visit a park, you may participate with the nature my imitating the animals. For example if a lion roars, you roar with the same type of sound. This may look crazy especially if some strangers are around you. Then you need to say it not too loud but if alone or with your friends don't feel ashamed. Just **SHOUT loudly** with the same sound of an animal. This is not only shouting but doing as the animals are doing. Monkeys can be so good to imitate especially when depressed. You know they are so funny. And imitating them you will end up laughing at yourself instead of being depressed.

11. Call for a Good friend

Sharing what you are going through with someone you trust especially during the onset of depression reduces your mind from depression with more than 30%. In other words you should first share with others what you are going through before it develops to suicidal thoughts

Also just as in the case of stress, the act of laughing helps your body fight stress in a number of ways. After you share, get to your bedroom and laugh at yourself. Stand at the mirror and laugh with your mirror image. Just as in stress remedies, I love myself remedy involves 4 steps:

➢ 1. Stand in front of a big mirror.
➢ 2. Read the piece of paper you wrote on remedy 3 as you are standing on a big mirror and while recording with a recorder For example say loudly; *"I feel like dying or killing myself."*

➢ 3. Ensure you are looking at yourself on the mirror as you read it through the whole piece of paper.

➢ 4. Now, as you stand on the mirror open the recorder and listen to yourself as you are facing the mirror.

By listening to yourself, will cause you laughing at yourself. And since you are looking at yourself in front of the mirror, will ADD up the laughter.

This may sound crazy but it reduces both stress and depression with a high capacity. I called it **'self humor'** **or "I love myself'** stress remedy because it's funny and it shows how you love yourself and that you love to be happy. Next thing you find is laughing like a crazy person but you aren't. Actually you are becoming better. This is very effective natural remedy to both stress and depression and I use it and laugh at myself and makes my day.

This remedy can be used even when not depressed to add up your happiness.

12. Take a long cold bath

Just as in the case of stress, water does a lot to relieve one from depression. This is what I term as **'psycho-hydrotherapy'**. Take a long bath especially with cold water. As much as it may depend on you, spend more time in the water. As I mentioned in the stress remedies, water is **'psychophilos'** meaning that you cannot separate the brain from water. They are always strong and loving friends.

13. Drink more warm water

Just as in the case of stress also drink more water especially warm in nature. It is also a good psychophilos for both stress and depression relief.

15. Get Foot Massage

Massaging can also do better especially on the feet as feet have reflexes or have nerves which are direct to the brain.

16. Listen to a Nice Cooling Music Daily

Just as in the case of stress, music especially religious songs which are played softly do a lot in natural treatment of depression. As I said in the stress remedies please be sure to select wisely the songs to play because some songs are depressants by themselves. For example listening to a rock song after losing your loved one or divorcing, may keep on adding your depression. Please play your music softly especially a spiritual song. Spiritual songs are spirit builders in nature.

17. Watch a Funny video or a Comedy

Now watching to a comedy will depend on what is depressing you. If it is something small like losing your phone or failure in exam, comedy may be good.

But for a bigger thing like losing a loved one it's better to listen to a nice cooling spiritual music.

18. Get enough Rest.

Depression causes some people not to have enough sleep.
Ensure you go to your bed the same time you are used to. Have
enough sleep. Sleep helps a lot in relaxing your mind. The more
you sleep the more the mind relaxes but be careful also not to
oversleep. Have at least 8 hours of sleep daily.

19. Spend time with others.

Spend time with positive people who influence your life
positively. When you spend time with those people you will feel
as if they are also sharing in your depression. Please be careful
of the people you spend with. Some might be more depressors
than your current depression. Be selective especially in times
like this.

20. Go for an exercise in the field

Exercise is one of the effective remedies to depression. As I have said earlier, brain needs enough oxygen especially when stressed or depressed. It is very important to feed it with enough oxygen as much as you can. This oxygen is highly necessary in breaking down the nutrients like glucose to energy to help the brain carry its many activities.

Aerobic exercise means that you will involve yourself in an activity or exercise which will involve FASTER AND FASTER BREATHING or INTAKE OF OXYGEN.

Exercise regularly and do it even more especially when depressed. If you love gym, it might be good. Also walking around your garden or outside your house quietly may help a lot.

21. Adopt Healthy Eating Lifestyle

Some people when depressed do not eat enough or never eat at all as I have indicated in the depression symptoms. It is important you eat as usual. Start with the breakfast. Eat enough breakfast, full of legumes, vegetable, nuts and collection of fruits. Eat enough like a big manager as if you are in the Garden of Eden. Please avoid at all coffee, tea, alcohol, bear, whine, sugar and any other caffeine related substances. These do a lot of harm to your body and may affect your sleep. Avoid alcohol, even though is rarely. It may promote depression.

You may also take a fresh fruits or vegetables or both fruits and vegetables juice. Make juice by yourself. Get collection of fruits, vegetables and juicer and make your own juice. This is very nice especially when suffering from depression. This is because your brain at this time requires enough energy as it's involved in a deep work.

As have said earlier, brain by itself requires about 20% out of the total oxygen inhaled. It also requires enough nutrients to help it carry out its many functions. Hence, at this time needs food which doesn't need a lot of time for digestion, absorption and respiration to provide energy. What I mean here is, when depressed, the brain needs food which can be converted to energy as fast as possible. Fresh fruits or vegetables juice doesn't need to go a long process of digestion as other foods.

You may prefer to drink more juice than even eating your other food. Drink more and more especially at this time.

Take fresh fruits or vegetables or both fruits and vegetables juice. Make juice by yourself. Get collection of fruits, vegetables and juicer and make your own juice. This is very nice especially when suffering from stress or depression.

Why? As I said earlier, brain is involved in many activities and these activities are served and or controlled by the brain 24 hours. It hence requires enough energy to do so. This energy comes from food you eat.

When depressed it is, therefore, very important you eat food which can be BROKEN DOWN to produce energy as fast as possible. This can be like fresh fruit juice which requires less or no digestion to be absorbed and taken to the brain areas especially the frontal lobe.

You should therefore, make juice by yourself which contains all nutrients so that to help the brain in this time of higher activity (depression).

It is like a lorry carrying a very heavy load on a mountain or hill climbing. It moves slowly and consumes more fuel than when on a slope getting down, right? Yea! It does. When brain is on a depression is like a heavy truck climbing a mountain over loaded. The engine requires more f**uel**, a need to **be cooled down with water.**

What I mean here is that give brain something which can be broken down into energy so fast like fresh fruit juice. Take some few glasses like 3, 4, or even 5 of fresh fruit juice when in depression.

22. Take It to Jesus

When depressed, so many negative thoughts come along the way in your mind, like you are not important and no one loves you, and others which may lead to self-hatred and feeling of committing suicide. But just remember who created you? God. The ultimate Being who understands what you go through and feels. He is the greatest helper in times of depression and problems and He can restore back your happiness.

God is our Creator and **Sustainer** and He understands all our problems. In this case when depressed spend quality time **meditating** about your spiritual life. Think about God, pray and do even sing a song. Sing any song which is related to God, even though you may not know any song, you can just say "thank you God for everything in my life." "Or I praise you Lord with all my problems."

He has promised to never leave you alone nor forsake you; Deuteronomy 31:6 "Be strong and courageous. Do not be afraid or terrified because of them, for the Lord your God goes with you; **He will never leave you nor forsake you.**

CHAPTER 6

A COMPLETE HEALTH AND HAPPINESS BY NATURE

Chapter Summary

The New Concept Of Health and Happiness By Nature

The Concept of NEWSTART and 'NATUREWAS'

The Meaning Of NEWSTART
  Elaboration of NEWSTART

The Concept of 'NATUREWAS' To Achieving Health and Happiness

The origin of NUREWAS

A-Z of Happiness (NATUREWAS IN ACTION)

23 Natural Remedies For achieving An Ultimate Health and Boosting your Happiness (An Extension of NATUREWAS)

Health by nature is **unlimited** in nature. It is boundless and goes beyond many ways not only relieving from pain or healing but assuring and ensuring your high degree of happiness. By choosing to spend some time with nature every day is a way of assuring your increase in happiness day by day.

Everyone can buy wealth but not everyone can buy happiness. Happiness is when you are contented in life, free from stress and depression when nothing is bothering you whether inside or outside. No diseases, no tension. Neither any psychological, social, physical nor spiritual obstacle on your way. Life is easy and free. The beginning of the 'Great and Secure Success (GSS). This is what I call absolute happiness.

The concept of NEWSTART has been a unique way of ensuring all individuals are living a better life and without or avoiding diseases. It is the law of applying NATURE to help people to enjoy a disease free life. NATUREWAS is a word I apply not to weaken NEWSTART concept but adapting it in a new and advanced way as we will be looking at in this chapter.

NEWSTART is an acronym derived from eight words and concepts to apply in life to achieve your ultimate health. The eight words and concepts are as follows;

N - Nutrition

E-Exercise

W-Water

S-Sunlight

T-Temperance

A-Air

R-Rest

T-Trusting In God

1. Nutrition

This means eating a balanced diet full of vegetables, fruits, nuts and cereals and avoiding animal products. This is one way of achieving health living and as I mentioned is also a lifestyle of conquering stress.

2. Exercise

Having a walk or jogging every day. Exercise just as I have mentioned earlier is so crucial in health and wellbeing of all mankind. Exercise may not involve running many miles away in a day, but you may choose to walk some miles away every day.

3. Water

Drinking enough water as I have mentioned earlier is not only a remedy to stress and depression free but also a way of achieving a complete health.

Drink at least 2 liters of water during winter and 3 or more during summer depending on the way your skin is losing much water.

4. Sunlight

Getting enough light especially early in the morning is a better way of helping or allowing your body bones to be strong. Just as sunlight is essential in production of food in plants through **photosynthesis**, sunlight is also essential in production or synthesis of **Vitamin D** in the skin of animals. When it is introduced to the skin it leads to synthesis of vitamin D which is crucial for bones development. Hence sunlight especially early morning one is so crucial in achieving health. Ensure you open your windows very early in the morning to allow enough and fresh light to enter and circulate the whole house's rooms.

5. Temperance

Temperance here refers to avoiding drugs and any chemical which might interfere with your health. These chemicals are like;

- Marijuana
- Tobacco
- Alcohol
- Caffeine
- Cocaine
- And many more.

6. Air

Oxygen is free. God is good that He supplies it free from the plants to all living animals. It is important you get enough of it by staying in an environment or a house well supplied with oxygen. Ensure your house windows are open during the day to allow free circulation of air in your rooms. As I mentioned eelier, your brain alone needs at least 20% of inhaled oxygen. Hence ensure you get enough fresh air daily.

7. Rest

Getting enough rest is not only one way of preventing or lowering you from cases of stress, depression and suicide but is also an ultimate way to achieving complete health and happiness. Ensure you sleep enough at night at least 8 hours per night for adults and more than 10 hours for children per night. Resting here does not only mean physical rest but also spiritual rest. Repenting your sins every day involves rest.

8. Trusting in God

Having faith in God that He can do greater things than a man can do. That He can take care of you and keep you away from illnesses. Trusting in God as I have mentioned many times is the most ultimate way of achieving health, wellbeing and happiness as we will see more in detail later in this chapter.

THE CONCEPT OF 'NATUREWAS' TO ACHIEVING HEALTH AND HAPPINESS

If you look at the application **NEWSTART** very carefully you will find that NEWSTART is a way of applying nature to achieve physical and spiritual health. By starting with;

- ✓ Nutrition
- ✓ Exercise
- ✓ Water
- ✓ Sunlight
- ✓ Temperance
- ✓ Air
- ✓ Rest and
- ✓ Trusting in God

seem to be a way of achieving purposely or primarily physical and spiritual health.

Health is not a complete health unless it involves the four holistic qualities:

- ✓ 1. Physical
- ✓ 2. Psychological
- ✓ 3. Social and
- ✓ 4. Spiritual.

By going through the concept of NEWSTART deeply and carefully I find that the second (Psychological) and third (Social) component of holistic quality of health and happiness is not fully stressed in.

For example if someone is feeling guilty, after has stolen from someone, neither;

- ☒ Nutrition
- ☒ Exercise
- ☒ Water
- ☒ Sunshine
- ☒ Temperance
- ☒ Rest or

is helpful at that moment to relieve that person from the guilt pain and suffering. This person who has stolen and as a result is feeling guilt has broken the third quality or aspect of health and happiness, the **'SOCIAL'** aspect. In this case to help someone who is going through this disorder, he is supposed to go first and return what he has taken from the other person. In other words, in order to achieve health and happiness, he or she must not only be physically fit but also socially fit as well.

And hence I developed a new concept for achieving HEALTH and HAPINNESS. This is not meant to weaken or disapprove the concept of NEWSTART but to advance it by putting some more components to help achieve health and happiness. This I called NATUREWAS' concept.

The concept of NATUREWAS (9 letters acronym) has the same meaning to NEWSTART (which IS 8 letters acronym) in many ways except the introduction of the social/psychological concept to achieving an ultimate health and happiness. Now let's look at the concept of NATUREWAS in relation to NEWSATART.

The Meaning of NATUREWAS

N- Nutrition

A-Air

T-Trusting In God

U-Unselfishness/Sharing (The SOCIAL aspect). Also

PSYCHOLOGICAL as it improves happiness.

R-Rest

E-Exercise

W-Water

A- Abstinence (Equivalence to Temperance in NEWSATART).

S-Sunlight

Elaboration of NATUREWAS

1. Nutrition

Just as in the concept of NEWSTART, this means eating a balanced diet full of;

- ✓ Vegetables
- ✓ Fruits
- ✓ Nuts
- ✓ Cereals
- ✓ Avoiding animal products
- ✓ Whole foods
- ✓ Balanced diet
- ✓ Etc.

This is one way of achieving health living and as I mentioned is also a lifestyle of conquering stress and depression.

2. Air

Just as in the concept of NEWSTART, everyone needs oxygen which is free. God is good that He supplies it free from the plants to all living animals. It is important you get enough of it by staying in an environment or a house well supplied with oxygen. Ensure your house windows are open during the day to allow free circulation of air in your rooms.

3. Trusting in God

Just as in the concept of NEWSTART, trusting in God as I have mentioned many times is the most ultimate way of achieving health, wellbeing and happiness as we will see more in detail later in this chapter.

4. Unselfishness

The concept of unselfishness here refers to thinking about welfare of other people as you think of yours. This is just as in the case of example I have used above. A person who has stolen it means that, he or she is selfish in nature. And due to his or her selfishness, ends up deteriorating his or her health, wellbeing and happiness through **guilt**. And therefore to achieve health and happiness everyone should be concerned with welfare of others. This involves sharing your belonging with the less fortunate people. In other words in order to achieve an ultimate health and happiness one has to be concerned not only on physical, (Nutrition, Exercise, Water, Sunshine, Temperance, Air and Rest)or Spiritual (Trusting in God) but should also be much concerned with welfare of other people which contributes to Social/Psychological aspect.

By being concerned with welfare of other people for example;

- ✓ Not wronging anyone
- ✓ Doing good things to others
- ✓ Maintaining a good relationship with others leads
- ✓ Helping others
- ✓ Being kind ore generous
- ✓ Asking for forgiveness when does wrong
- ✓ Etc,

 reduce or ends guilt, stress, and depression. And hence leads to achievement of **PSYCHOLOGICAL health** (The second quality or aspect of health and happiness). For example guilt is a disorder which is as a result of break down of SOCIAL aspect of health. One feels guilty when does wrong to others or himself. And by feeling guilty, may lead to someone developing a psychological problems like stress, depression and anxiety.

Hence, SOCIAL aspect of health and happiness has a very close relationship to the second aspect, the PSYCHOLOGICAL aspect.

In other words in order to achieve a complete health, wellbeing and happiness, we must avoid **SELFISHNESS.** We must not only think of bettering our lives but others too. We must think of others too in all ways.

5. Rest

Just as in the concept of NEWSTART, getting enough rest is not only one way of preventing or lowering you from cases of stress, depression and suicide but is also an ultimate way to achieving complete health and happiness. As I said earlier, ensure you sleep enough at night at least 8 hours per night for adults and more than 10 hours for children per night. Again, resting here does not only mean physical rest but also spiritual rest, that is, repenting your sins every day and being close to God.

6. Exercise

Just as in the concept of NEWSTART, having enough exercise just as I have mentioned earlier is so crucial in health and wellbeing of all mankind. Exercise may not involve running many miles away in a day, but you may choose to walk some miles away every day.

7. Water

Just as in the concept of NEWSTART, drinking enough water as I have mentioned earlier is not only a remedy to stress and depression free but also a way of achieving a complete health.

Drink at least 2 liters of water during winter and 3 or more during summer depending on the way your skin is losing much water.

8. Abstinence

This is equivalence to Temperance in NEWSTART. And here abstinence refers to avoiding drugs and any chemical which might interfere with your health. These chemicals are like;

- Alcohol
- Caffeine
- Marijuana
- Tobacco
- Cocaine
- And many more.

 Abstaining from this kind of chemicals gives the body a chance only to focus on health nutrition in **N** letter hence, equipping and giving the body enough energy which in returns leads to happier life.

9. Sunlight

Just as in the concept of NEWSTART, getting enough light especially early in the morning is a better way of helping or allowing your body bones to be strong. Just as sunlight is essential in production of food in plants through photosynthesis, sunlight is also essential in production or synthesis of Vitamin D in the skin of animals. When it is introduced to the skin it leads to synthesis of vitamin D which is crucial for bones development. Hence sunlight especially early morning one is so crucial in achieving health. Ensure you open your windows very early in the morning to allow enough and fresh light to enter and circulate the whole house's rooms.

THE ORIGIN OF NUREWAS

This acronym I developed and called it since the nature was and has been existing since creation and has a remedy given by God Himself to human being in Genesis 1 to prevent and cure human being diseases and illness. And as I mentioned, God created man and woman with a purpose of human being to depend and rely in Him as well as on nature. Nature in Genesis 1:29 which involve natural foods like;

- ✓ Vegetables
- ✓ Fruits
- ✓ Nuts
- ✓ Water

✓ Etc,

is seen as the first natural doctor to human being preventing and curing many illness. And, therefore, **NATURE WAS** since the creation acting as a natural doctor to human kind.

During the creation and many more years later, there has been neither artificial medicine nor doctor as it is seen today. These artificial medicine and doctors came later or recently but the NATURE WAS since the creation as a natural medicine and natural doctor to human kind.

Therefore, NATUREWAS and it is and will always be there even in NEW EARTH, Revelation 22.

If we can look at the book of Revelation 22 in the bible, it mentions that in new heaven there will be the following:

> A river and
> Water of life
> A tree of life on each side of the river
> 12 crops of fruit and
> A fruit every month
> Leaves of the tree are for healing of nations

This means that God will have restored the earth to as it was in Garden of Eden. This is an **hint** to tell all of us that in the new heaven no need of priests and medical doctors any more for **THE LAMB OF GOD** and the **NATURE** will serve that. And this is also a hint that **happiness** which will be forever facilitated by nature (e.g. River of life, Tree of life, **Healing leaves**). Look at the use of healing leaves. This means the nature will be at its original work and purpose of HEALING in that there will be;

- ✓ No more Death
- ✓ No more mourning
- ✓ No more crying
- ✓ No more Pain
- ✓ For the old order of things has passed away

What am trying to say is that nature since the beginning is not only meant for healing and prevention but also for Happiness and this will be even in the NEW EARTH.

It has been there always since the creation. Before the modern day artificial medicines and doctors came to exist, NATURE WAS existing since creation. Hence, NATURE WAS (NATUREWAS).

Though we live in a world of stress, depression and pain, among other problems in life, we can still conquer all and attain our ultimate happiness. But how? The question comes. It is very easy as we have been seeing from the beginning of this book.

By utilizing nature and allowing God to be part of our lives we can attain an ultimate happiness in life. Now let's look at many ways we can overcome many obstacles of life and become happier in life.

Sky Walk

1. Have Sky Walk (Night Walk) Daily

Have a night walk which I termed as sky walk daily. Having a walk alone and trying to breathe deeply in and out can boost your body pleasure higher than normal and help to reduce work tension that you had during the day.

The best walk is usually at night but if you get time in the morning can also help your body achieve pleasure and happiness. When you are slightly walking at night, always walk looking at the sky; the stars, moon, clouds and the beauty of heaven. This helps much to connect you with the sky nature and beauty boosting your happiness to a higher level. Usually, it is more pleasurable if you do it with you husband, wife or a close friend.

Exercise

2. Go for an exercise in the field daily

Before the sky walk at night, its better you have an exercise day time for some time. Exercise regularly and if you love gym, it might be good. Also walking around your garden or outside your house quietly may help a lot in boosting your energy and happiness.

The exercise does much in boosting one's happiness. Not only does it promote good health, but it promotes good behavior especially which promotes happiness, reduces tension and lowers sadness.

The fact is that happiness and health go hand in hand. The more you are healthy, the more you are likely to be more happier in life. The more you are happier in life the more you are likely to have a better health.

3. Change your Daily Leisure at least once in a week

This means that if you are used to have your dinner at home every day, you may once in a week visit your best friend and have dinner with him/her. By changing your daily leisure time will motivate you to a new way of life rather than you are used to. This will also prevent you from staying in one place and allows you to be more interactive and happier.

4. Adopt Health Eating Lifestyle

Eat a balanced diet daily. Start with the breakfast. Eat enough breakfast, full of legumes, vegetable, nuts and collection of fruits. Eat enough like a big manager as if you are in your own rich garden.

The real secret behind happiness in many people and families is their LIFESTYLE;

- ✓ The way you live
- ✓ What you do every day
- ✓ How you think about things

- ✓ How you respond to different threats in life
- ✓ Your morality
- ✓ What you eat
- ✓ What you drink
- ✓ And many more

are all that determines your maximum happiness.

This is the secret which I follow every day in life and find myself being happier in life and avoiding many life threats hence facilitating my happiness.

Abstinence /Temperance

5. Avoid or Abstain from harmful foods and chemicals

Any food that you really know that does not promote a good health, it's better to abstain from it. Sometimes it's hard to do so but it is helpful and beneficial for your own health and happiness.

The fact is that, one of the threats in life which cause many people to spend life unhappy is sicknesses. But when people are free from diseases, this adds up to their happiness. And, therefore, as I have said earlier, please avoid at all;

- Cocaine
- Coffee
- Tea
- Alcohol
- Beer
- Whine
- Tobacco
- Sugar
- And any other caffeine related substances.

These do a lot of harm to your body and may affect your health. Avoid alcohol, even though is rarely. By doing this your body will always be energized hence boosting your happiness. If it is possible as far as it may depend on you, avoid animal products like,

- Meat,
- Chicken,
- Eggs
- Etc.

Natural food as we have already seen i.e. food from plants is the best food and source of energy which boosts your happiness.

6. Look at everything in a Positive way

Always look at everything in a positive way by trying to know that life is always ups and downs. Today you may face a problem but that problem is not there to stay. Be calm always and try to be positive in all things. Avoid negative thoughts by spending time with the word of God.

7. Conquer Suicidal Thinking

In cases where you may feel life is really threatening, try to stay close and be connected to God and good friends. This will help you avoid suicidal thinking. Try always not to stay alone. Always think of mixing with others. This will help you challenge the poor thoughts.

8. Take a long cold bath at least twice in a day

Ensure in the morning and evening you take bath just when you wake up and before sleeping respectively. As I said earlier, water does a lot to relieve one from many tensions. This is what I termed as **'psycho-hydrotherapy'**. Take a long bath especially with cold water. As much as it may depend on you, spend more time in the water. As I mentioned in the stress remedies, water is **'psychophilos'** meaning that you cannot separate the brain from water. They are always strong and loving friends. Cold water is better but if is in the winter you may use warm water. This will always keep you away from many tensions and boosts your happiness daily.

9. Drink more warm water

 Just as in the case of stress and depression, drink more water especially warm in nature. It is also a good psychophilos for reducing tensions and boosting your happiness. Warm water is quite nice especially when it's cold. You may prefer cool water during summer and high temperature periods or seasons. The more you drink a lot of water, the more you are sure to fight against sadness and hence promoting happiness.

10. Listen to a Nice Cooling Music Daily

Listen to a cool and spirit building music daily especially when you wake up and before you go to bed. The best are religious songs which are played softly and can do a lot in relieving you from tensions and help boosting your happiness. Please play your music softly especially a spiritual song. Spiritual songs are spirit builders in nature. Always be sure to choose the songs to play very carefully. Some songs promote sadness in nature. For example assume you feel sad because of broken relationship. In this case listening to a love or romantic song may promote or increase your sadness as it will remind or convince you that you should be at the same mood with your love. And since you are already in a broken relationship currently, this can lead to crying, self hating etc. as the music reminds you about the best times you shared with your loved one but you aren't in that moment at the moment. The right song to play at this time is **spirit builder like a gospel song** which is meant to promote encouragement to your spirit but not reminding you of tensions and troubles of life.

11. Get enough Rest Daily

Sleep enough daily. Ensure you go to your bed the same time you are used to. Have enough sleep. Sleep helps a lot in relaxing your mind. The more you sleep the more the mind relaxes but also remember to be careful not to oversleep. Have at least 8 hours of sleep daily if you are an adult or old age, and at least 10 hours if a child. (Refer the exact amount to sleep in my book *"60 Natural Remedies to Guilt, Anxiety, Sleep Loss & Sadness").* This will ensure your body is always energized boosting your happiness every day.

Having enough sleep help your body to generate energy which will make you to wake up the next day joyful, happy and cheerful ready to face the day ahead and helps to keep your mood level high. Wherever you go, you have to tell yourself or someone this acronym I formed, **"SIH"** i.e. 'Sleep Is Happiness.'

12. Spend time with others daily

Spend time with positive people who influence your life positively and who make you feel important and special. When you spend time with those people you will feel as if they are also part of your life especially when in pain. If you want to be happy in life spend more time with these people.

 But also remember you also need time to create your new works and any other activities. As you spend more time with others you also should have your personal limits. Set amount of time to spend with your good friends. Be strict on that. Do not exceed the set time. Spending more time with others than the time you should be creating something new is not wise enough. Though you need to be happy with friends, you need time to create something new. When you create something new, which even others haven't created increases your happiness even more than the happiness from your friends. Always remember to set enough time for yourself.

For example observing how nice magazine or an article you have created and published can give you more happiness. Always think of creating something new.

13. Spend Enough Time focusing on your relationships

As I mentioned earlier in this book about **relationship stressors,** many people today are going through many sadness as a result of **relationship barriers**. Men and Women can be happier in life if they can conquer this threat. Most of people seem to be unhappy in life mainly because their relationships don't work.

After doing my research by asking women about whether they are happy in life, most of them who said they were happy said that it was because their relationship was fine while unhappy said they were facing relationship problems. As I mentioned earlier in my books like, *"Woman's Mind Innermost Hidden Secrets,"*, in the cause of prostitution and pornography, most of the women who had engaged in prostitution said that they were experiencing broken relationships like;

- Being widowed
- Broken love
- Divorced
- Infidelity from the husbands

➢ And many more

relationship failures which turned them to choose to revenge into commercial sex.

It is, therefore, wise enough to daily focus on your relationship and see how you can turn it to happiness. This includes spending a quality time with your;

✓ Family
✓ Children
✓ Husband
✓ Wife
✓ Parents
✓ Loved one
✓ Discussing your sexual life with your marriage partner and
✓ Looking for all ways to improve your relationship.

Spend enough time your loved one, wife or husband. Value the time you spend together discussing about;

➢ Life failures and drawbacks
➢ Life successes and progresses and
➢ Looking in all ways to improve at least something step ahead every day.

This is a wise way of chasing sadness and welcoming happiness especially in your relationship.

Personal Meditation

14. Self-Meditation

Sometimes create time to meditate and think about yourself. Think about your good things and experiences in the past in. Try and think of wishing to have the same or better experiences in the future.

Self-meditation or introspection helps much in appreciating the far you have come from. Thinking about how you;

- ✓ Escaped an accident
- ✓ How you got a wonderful husband
- ✓ How you got a wonderful wife
- ✓ How you got a wonderful girlfriend
- ✓ How you got a wonderful boyfriend
- ✓ How really God has blessed you with wonderful children
- ✓ Or how He has kept you alive till present
- ✓ Etc,

is one thing which can add up your joy and empower your happiness. Self meditation can be so good if done daily at any time.

15. Be More Hospitable and avoid Selfishness

The biggest mystery behind the happiness, is giving. Being kind to people as well as being hospitable gives a new special way to people turning your pain to joy and or happiness. Those who find themselves giving eventually find themselves happy and joyful mysteriously. The secret of giving is that, you give properties but in return people give you happiness. Never think of being selfish. Overcome evil by becoming good. Overcome sadness by becoming selfless.

Self Satisfaction

16. Be Self Contented

One of the ultimate ways of achieving happiness is trying always to be contented and satisfied with whatever little you have. If you have a small car, just be happy that you have, some people never even have a bicycle.

Learn to be satisfied with what you have. Your wife no matter how she looks like. Your husband, no matter the way he looks like. Your children. Food and even shelter. The little money that you have. Self contentment is another ideal and easy way to welcome happiness to your life and family.

This is also applicable to beauty. It's quite amazing knowing that you are naturally beautiful or handsome. And no matter what or when, no one could remove that thought from you.

 Self satisfaction of yourself is one of the **top remedies to achieving happiness** in life.

Smile

17. Smile even if things are wrong

Smiles cover many pains. Smile but also remember if you are unhappy smiling alone is not enough. Share your feeling with someone you trust. As I mentioned in this book in the case of stress, sharing is the best practice and remedy of throwing hurts and pains out of your mind. Smile then after sharing.

18. Self-Thinking Happiness

Say that it's not only you who is going through that painful experience. There are many more in the world going through the same pain. No human can be happy always. Sometimes some pains come but with trust in God they wither away soon.

This is a Positive self comparison in that, you compare your miseries in life and consider them to be too small as compared to bigger miseries happening to many people.

For example in the bible we have miseries of Job (Job chapter 1). Assume you have lost your son or daughter. Positive self comparison is that asking a question like; I LOST MY SON/DAUGHTER and am this depressed, WHAT ABOUT JOB WHO LOST ALL HIS CHILDREN? AND WHAT DID HE SAY? "NAKED I CAME AND NAKED SHALL I RETURN, PRAISE BE THE NAME OF THE LORD.

Positive Self Comparison or what I termed in Depression therapies as **Positive Self Comparison Therapy PSCT** is very effective remedy to happiness as one feels is **at least better** with smaller misery he/she has at the moment as compared to those who had, have or are experiencing worse than that.

19. Avoid Guilt and Anxiety

Try and avoid guilt as much as possible. This can be achieved by doing to others and yourself what is good and can make them feel well about you. By asking for forgiveness to your past sins and restarting your life new with God helps much in conquering guilt and developing a good and happy feelings.

At the same time avoiding anxiety by staying calm and relaxed, knowing that you cannot change the fate is another way of helping you become happier in life. Worries are one of the problems leading many people to poor health and sadness. Try always to avoid them.

20. Do What Is Right and avoid Evil

Another secret to more happiness in life and actually which is the secret behind plenty of happiness in addition to eating and drinking lifestyle is, MORALITY. By doing what is right and even teaching others to do the same, is the additional secret behind much happiness in life. By doing what is right and avoiding evil are two obligations which go hand in hand.

- ✓ 1. Doing good and
- ✓ 2. Avoiding evil.

By doing this does not only add up happiness to your life but also keeps you away from guilt which I have spoken of in the remedy 19 and hence, your mind and heart remain clean and happier.

As I mentioned earlier that " Disobedience is the root of all immorality and the immorality is the root of all pain." Always do what is right and you will avoid many sad instances in life.

Remember to do what is right always and avoid evil and you will never suffer from guilt which brings inner pain and unhappiness.

Avoid evil and do what is right, Amos 5:14 (text from the bible), "Seek good, and not evil, that ye may live; and so Jehovah, the God of hosts, will be with you, as ye say."

21. Have enough and clean air and sunlight Daily

By allowing natural light and air penetrate to your house from early morning till evening gives a chance that when you come to sleep at night, you can sleep in a room of fresh natural air and fresh atmosphere which had natural light throughout the day. This gives your body a fresh atmosphere at night which will keep your sleep at a better level. The better sleep you get at night will lead to your freshness and energy in the morning boosting your mind and body and strengthening it hence becoming more energized and happier in the next day.

22. Spending Time with the Nature

Try and visit natural places like rivers, lakes, mountains, trees and try to imagine being part of the nature, by participating with what that nature does. For example, if you visit a lake or a river, try and put your legs in the water, and feel the movements. You may also visit a swimming pool and spend sometime in the water. But be careful with yourself especially if you are so young or you don't know how to swim. This feeling get sensed by your legs, hands, body and is sent to your brain through sensory nerves which covers the whole of your body, leading to ease feeling and joy in your brain and your whole body, therefore, boosting your happiness.

Another example of the nature is going out for;

- ✓ A tour
- ✓ Walking around the beach
- ✓ Or visiting the park and
- ✓ Seeing the natural creations
- ✓ Spending time in the flower garden
- ✓ Smelling the beautiful flowers
- ✓ Seeing beautiful birds, insects like butterflies
- ✓ Etc,

can do much in to a reminder that you are part of that nature.

Nature is friendly and even if you feel hated, when spending time with nature like animals, flowers, birds helps one to recover naturally and feels important. The nature provides a special happiness and healing power from God of heaven and is one of the most ultimate sources of happiness power and, therefore, I put it close to the 23rd, the last most effective natural remedy to achieving happiness, "God."

23. Trusting in God

The Lord is the ultimate joy and happiness to all. He feels our pains, carry us to a happy breeze and we are restful.

David says in Psalms 63:5-7 (Text from the bible) "My soul will be satisfied as with fat and rich food, and my mouth will praise you with joyful lips, when I remember you upon my bed, and meditate on you in the watches of the night; for you have been my help, and in the shadow of your wings I will sing for joy."

Being close to God as well as doing what is right is an ultimate way to be happy in life. God loves His people and is happy when we all are happy. His purpose and aim is to see us happy and even happier in this life as well as the life to come.

Trust and obey Him every day and He will surely sustain and increase your happiness.

BIBLIOGRAPHY

Note: Most of the research in this book I did personally and face to face from men and women by the help of my new system in Psychology, 'Psychemoanalysis' where I had developed a HMQ test. The method I applied in doing my face to face research was; field survey, case study, observation, interviews, and questionnaires, and psychemotherapies including online. The rest of the research I compared my personal research with, the bible, and others researchers and psychologists from some/all of the following few sources:

Biblestudytools.com/amos/5-14-compare html Depression Health Center

Bookstore.mayoclinic.com/products/books/Details.
cfm?mpid=61&trkid=21242S198705050

Edition.cnn. health/nine-happiness-tips/index
En.m.wikipedia.org/wiki/Anxiety

Ginny O'Brien 2008

www.columbiaconsult.com/pubs/v52_fall07.htm

Godvine.com/bible/amos/5-15

Healthysleep.med harvard.edu/healthy/getting/overcoming/tips

McLeod, S. A. (2013). In www.

simplypsychology.org/Sigmund-Freud.html

Psychcentral.com/blog/archives/2007/11/27/5-tips-for-dealing-with-guilt/

Simplypsychology.org/Sigmund-Freud.html

Webmd.com/default.htm

Classic Books for a Better Lifestyle and excellent Future by A life changing Author.

www.ingramcontent.com/pod-product-compliance
Lightning Source LLC
Chambersburg PA
CBHW070921290526
45795CB00001B/380